THE NOVELLO
BOOK OF DESCANTS

34 DESCANTS TO THE BEST-LOVED HYMNS

SELECTED AND EDITED BY CHRISTOPHER ROBINSON

NOVELLO

FRONT COVER St. George's Chapel, Windsor (Tim Graham/Corbis)

MUSIC SETTING Chris Hinkins

NOV956021 (Full music edition)
ISBN 978-1-84772-252-2
NOV956021-01 (Descant book. Pack of ten copies)

HEAD OFFICE
14/15 Berners Street,
London W1T 3LJ
Tel. +44 (0)20 7612 7400
Fax +44 (0)20 7612 7545

SALES AND HIRE
Hal Leonard Europe Limited,
Newmarket Road,
Bury St Edmunds,
Suffolk IP33 3YB
England
Tel +44 (0)1284 702600
Fax +44 (0)1284 768301

www.chesternovello.com

Other anthologies for upper voices available from Novello:

High Praise NOV032118
High Praise 2 NOV020680
Merrily on High NOV032121

Contents

Preface

In the twelfth century the word *discantus* denoted an improvised counterpoint sung above a plainsong. A more recent precursor of the modern descant was the faux bourdon as found in Ravenscroft's Psalter (1621). The best example is Dowland's setting of the Old Hundredth, later used by Vaughan Williams in his stirring version of that hymn.

The main purpose of a descant is to provide variety, and more particularly to add an extra frisson to the last verse of a hymn. It is essentially a decoration and should not dominate or distract. Some general remarks about performance may be helpful.

(1) There is no need to over-sing a descant, particularly when the tessitura is high. An unyielding fortissimo is tiresome.

(2) It is often effective to ask the tenors to double the descant, thereby creating a fuller choral texture (Nos. 6 and 13 are obvious exceptions).

(3) A robust organ sound is required with enough foundation tone to provide the necessary harmonic richness.

Christopher Robinson
Cambridge, June 2007

1. Angel-voices ever singing

ANGEL VOICES

E.G. Monk (1819–1900)
arr. Christopher Robinson (b.1936)

Francis Pott (1832–1909)

2. All my hope on God is founded

MICHAEL

Herbert Howells (1892–1983)

- known calls my heart._____ Christ_____ doth

gift of Christ his Son. Christ doth call One and___

call:_____ Ye who fol - low___ shall___ not fall.

all: Ye who fol - low shall___ not fall.

Robert Bridges (1844–1930),
based on the German of J. Neander (1650–80)

3. Christ is made the sure foundation (I)

WESTMINSTER ABBEY

Henry Purcell (1659–95), adapted
arr. Christopher Robinson

5

Latin 7th century,
tr. J.M. Neale (1818–66)

4. Christ is made the sure foundation (II)

WESTMINSTER ABBEY

Henry Purcell (1659–95), adapted
arr. Barry Rose (b.1934)

Choir in harmony or unison

Latin 7th century,
tr. J.M. Neale (1818–66)

5. Come down, O Love divine

DOWN AMPNEY

R. Vaughan Williams (1872–1958)
arr. Christopher Robinson

And so the yearn - ing___ strong,

And so the yearn - ing strong,

With which the soul___ will___ long, Shall far out - pass the

With which the soul___ will long, Shall far out - pass the

Bianco da Siena (d.1434),
tr. R.F. Littledale (1833–90)

6. Abide with me

EVENTIDE

W.H. Monk (1823–89)
arr. Christopher Robinson

DESCANT (SOPRANO)

MELODY

ORGAN

Hold thou the cross be - fore my clos-ing eyes; Shine through the

Hold thou the cross be - fore my clos-ing eyes; Shine through the

gloom, and point me to the skies: Heaven's mor-ning breaks, and

gloom, and point me to the skies: Heaven's mor-ning breaks, and

earth's vain sha-dows flee; In life, in death, O Lord, a - bide with me.

earth's vain sha-dows flee; In life, in death, O Lord, a - bide with me.

H.F. Lyte (1793–1847)

7. Come, thou long-expected Jesus

CROSS OF JESUS

John Stainer (1840–1901)
arr. Christopher Robinson

Charles Wesley (1707–88)

8. Eternal Monarch, King most high

GONFALON ROYAL

P.C. Buck (1871–1947)
arr. Christopher Robinson

DESCANT

O＿ ri-sen Christ, a-scend-ed Lord, All＿ praise to

MELODY

O ri - sen Christ, a - scend-ed Lord,＿＿ All praise to

ORGAN

thee＿ let earth ac - cord, Who art, while end - less a - ges run, With

thee let earth ac - cord, Who art, while end - less a - ges run, With

Fa - ther and with Spi - rit One. A - - - men.

Fa - ther＿ and with Spi - rit One. A - - - men.

Latin 5th century,
tr. J.M. Neale (1818–66)

9. Good Christian men, rejoice and sing

VULPIUS (GELOB'T SEI GOTT)

melody from Vulpius's *Gesangbuch*, Jena 1609
arr. Christopher Robinson

Cyril Alington (1872–1955)

10. For all the Saints who from their labours rest

SINE NOMINE

R. Vaughan Williams (1872–1958)
arr. Christopher Robinson

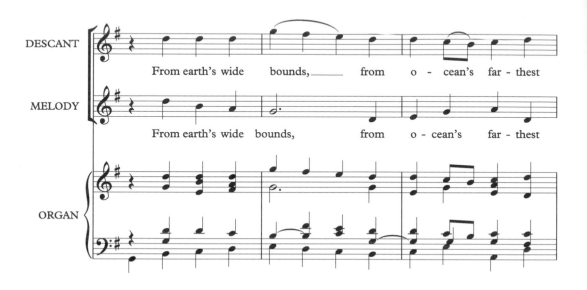

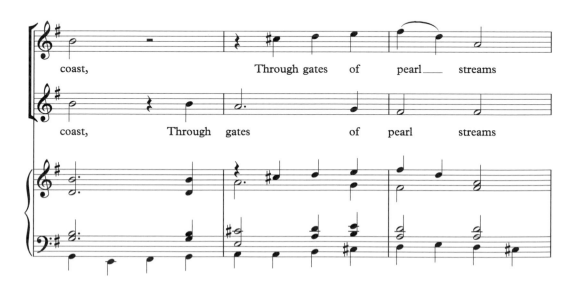

W. Walsham How (1823–97)

11. Glorious things of thee are spoken

ABBOT'S LEIGH

Cyril V. Taylor (1907–91)
arr. Christopher Robinson

John Newton (1725–1807)

18

12. Hark! the herald angels sing

BERLIN

Felix Mendelssohn (1809–47)
arr. Christopher Robinson

Charles Wesley (1707–88)

13. Holy Spirit, ever dwelling

SALISBURY

Herbert Howells (1892–1983)
arr. Christopher Robinson

Timothy Rees (1874–1939)

14. Holy, Holy, Holy! Lord God Almighty

NICAEA

J.B. Dykes (1823–76)
arr. Christopher Robinson

Reginald Heber (1783–1826)

15. Let all mortal flesh keep silence

PICARDY

17th century French carol
arr. Sidney Campbell (1909–74)

Liturgy of St. James,
tr. Gerard Moultrie (1829–85)

16. Lo! he comes with clouds descending

HELMSLEY

melody noted by Thomas Olivers (1725–99),
from Wesley's *Select Hymns with Tunes Annex'd*
arr. Christopher Robinson

Charles Wesley (1707–88)

17. Lord, enthroned in heavenly splendour

ST HELEN

George Martin (1844–1916)
arr. Christopher Robinson

DESCANT

MELODY

ORGAN

Life-im-part-ing heaven-ly Man-na, Strick-en Rock with stream-ing side,

Heaven and earth with loud ho-san-na Wor-ship thee, the Lamb who died,

Al - le-lu - ia, al - le-lu - ia, Risen, as-cend-ed, glo - ri-fied!

G.H. Bourne (1840–1925)

18. O worship the King

HANOVER

melody by William Croft (1678–1727)
arr. Christopher Robinson

DESCANT
O mea-sure-less Might, In - ef - fa - ble Love, While an - gels de-

MELODY
O mea-sure-less Might, In - ef - fa - ble Love, While an - gels de-

ORGAN

-light___ To hymn thee a - bove, Thy hum - bler cre - a - tion, Though

-light To hymn thee_ a - bove, Thy hum - bler cre - a - tion, Though

fee - ble their lays, With true a - do - ra - tion Shall sing to thy praise.

fee - ble their lays, With true a - do - ra - tion Shall sing to thy praise.

Robert Grant (1779–1838)

19. Love Divine, all loves excelling

BLAENWERN

William Rowlands (1860–1937)
arr. Christopher Robinson

Charles Wesley (1707–88)

20. Mine eyes have seen the glory

BATTLE HYMN

melody by J.W. Steffe
descant by Ralph Allwood (b.1950)

Julia Ward Howe (1819–1910),
and others

21. My song is love unknown

LOVE UNKNOWN

John Ireland (1879–1962)
arr. Christopher Robinson

Samuel Crossman (1624–83)

22. Now thank we all our God (I)

NUN DANKET

melody in J. Crüger's *Praxis Pietatis Melica*, c.1647
descant by George Guest (1924–2002)

them in high-est hea - ven, The One e - ter - nal

them in high-est hea - ven, The One e - ter - nal

God, Whom earth and heaven a - dore; For

God, Whom earth and heaven a - dore; For

thus it was, is now, And shall be e - ver - more.

thus it was, is now, And shall be e - ver - more.

Martin Rinkart (1586–1649),
tr. Catherine Winkworth (1827–78)

23. Now thank we all our God (II)

NUN DANKET

melody in J. Crüger's *Praxis Pietatis Melica,* c.1647
arr. Christopher Robinson

Martin Rinkart (1586–1649),
tr. Catherine Winkworth (1827–78)

24. O come, all ye faithful (I)

ADESTE FIDELES

18th century melody?
descant by J. Roland Middleton (1896–1983)

DESCANT

Yea, Lord, we greet thee, Born this hap-py morn - ing,

MELODY

Yea, Lord, we greet thee, Born this hap-py morn - ing,

ORGAN

Je - su,_ to thee_ be glo - ry giv'n;

Je - su, to thee_____ be glo - ry giv'n;

Word of the Fa - ther, Now in flesh ap - pear - ing:

Word of the Fa - ther, Now in flesh ap - pear - ing: O

O come, O

come let us a - dore him, O come let us a - dore him, O

come let us a - dore him, Christ the Lord.

come let us a - dore him, Christ the Lord.

Latin 18th century,
tr. Frederick Oakley (1802–80) and others

25. O come, all ye faithful (II)

ADESTE FIDELES

18th century melody?
arr. Christopher Robinson

DESCANT

MELODY

ORGAN

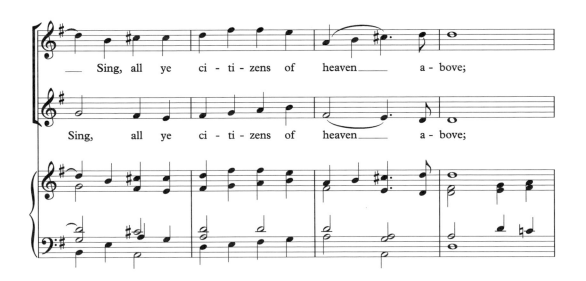

Glo-ry to God in the high-est: O come, let us a-dore him, let us a-dore him, let us a-dore him Christ the Lord.

Glo-ry to God in the high-est: O come, let us a-dore him, O come, let us a-dore him, O come, let us a-dore him Christ the Lord.

Latin 18th century,
tr. Frederick Oakley (1802–80) and others

26. On Jordan's bank the Baptist's cry

WINCHESTER NEW

adapted from a chorale in *Musikalisches Hand-Buch*
Hamburg 1690
arr. Barry Rose

DESCANT

All praise, e - ter - nal Son, to thee Whose

MELODY

All praise, e - ter - nal Son, to thee Whose

ORGAN

ad - vent sets thy peo - ple free, A - dore,_____

ad - vent sets thy peo - ple free, Whom, with the Fa - ther,

_____ And Spi - rit blest, for e - ver - more.

we a - dore, And Spi - rit blest, for e - ver - more.

Charles Coffin (1676–1749),
tr. John Chandler

27. Once in Royal David's City

IRBY

H.J. Gauntlett (1805–76)
arr. Christopher Robinson

C.F. Alexander (1818–95)

28. Praise, my soul, the King of heaven

PRAISE MY SOUL

John Goss (1800–80)
arr. Christopher Robinson

moon, bow down be - fore him, dwell - ers all in
moon, bow down be - fore him, dwell - ers all in

time and space. Praise him! Praise him! Praise
time and space. Praise him! Praise him! Praise him!

him! Praise with us the God of grace.
Praise him! Praise with us the God of grace.

H.F. Lyte (1793–1847)

29. Ride on! ride on in majesty

WINCHESTER NEW

adapted from a chorale in *Musikalisches Hand-Buch*
Hamburg 1690
arr. Christopher Robinson

Charles Coffin (1676–1749),
tr. John Chandler

30. The day thou gavest, Lord, is ended

ST CLEMENT

Clement Scholefield (1839–1904)
arr. Christopher Robinson

John Ellerton (1826–93)

31. Thou whose almighty word

MOSCOW

adapted from a tune by F. Giardini (1716–96)
arr. Christopher Robinson

DESCANT
MELODY
ORGAN

Bless-èd and ho - ly Three, Glo - ri - ous Tri - ni -

-ty, Wis-dom, Love, Might, Bound-less as o-cean's tide Roll-ing in

full - est pride, Through the world far and wide Let there be light.

John Marriott (1780–1825)

32. Through the night of doubt and sorrow

MARCHING

Martin Shaw (1875–1958)
arr. Christopher Robinson

Bernhardt Ingemann (1789–1862),
tr. S. Baring-Gould (1834–1924)

33. Unto us is born a son

PUER NOBIS

melody from *Piae Cantiones* (1582)
arr. Christopher Robinson

tr. G.R. Woodward (1848–1934)

34. When I survey the wondrous cross

ROCKINGHAM

adapted by Edward Miller (1731–1807)
descant by George Guest

Isaac Watts (1674–1748)